CONFIDENCE-BUILDING ACTIVITIES FOR MINECRAFTERS

AN UNOFFICIAL GUIDE

MORE THAN 50 ACTIVITIES TO HELP KIDS LEVEL UP THEIR SELF-ESTEEM!

ERIN FALLIGANT

Sky Pony Press
New York

Copyright © 2020 by Hollan Publishing, Inc.

Minecraft® is a registered trademark of Notch Development AB.

The Minecraft game is copyright © Mojang AB.

Sky Pony Press books may be purchased in bulk at special discounts for sales promotion, corporate gifts, fund-raising, or educational purposes. Special editions can also be created to specifications. For details, contact the Special Sales Department, Sky Pony Press, 307 West 36th Street, 11th Floor, New York, NY 10018 or info@skyhorsepublishing.com.

Sky Pony® is a registered trademark of Skyhorse Publishing, Inc.®, a Delaware corporation.

Minecraft® is a registered trademark of Notch Development AB. The Minecraft game is copyright © Mojang AB.

Visit our website at www.skyponypress.com.

10 9 8 7 6 5 4 3 2 1

Library of Congress Cataloging-in-Publication Data is available on file.

Print ISBN: 978-1-5107-6190-2

Cover design by Brian Peterson
Interior design by Noora Cox
Cover and interior illustrations by Amanda Brack

Printed in China

DEAR MINECRAFTER,

What is confidence? It's knowing who you are and all the amazing things you can do. It's feeling good about yourself most of the time, and knowing how to make yourself feel better even on bad days. It's believing in yourself and knowing that if you really try, you can do almost anything!

Just as you mine for blocks in Minecraft, there are ways to "mine" for confidence. This book will show you how, with fun challenges, puzzles, and fill-in-the-blank adventures. As you explore the Overworld with your favorite characters and critters, you'll gain tools you can use in the real world too. With every page, you'll feel a little happier, stronger, and more confident.

Ready to begin? Grab your pickaxe—er, pencil—and let's get started!

CONTENTS

THE ONE AND ONLY YOU

Imagine a world where everyone looks and acts exactly the same. How boring would that be? Our differences make us interesting!

Circle the two villagers below who look exactly the same.

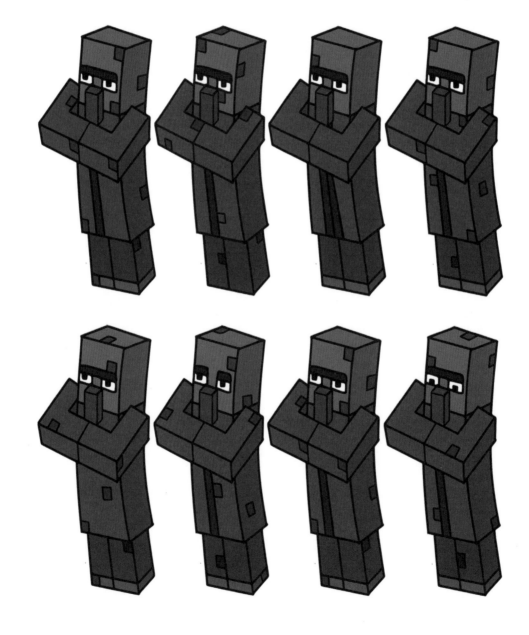

That was tough, right? In the real world, no two people are exactly alike.

What makes you unique? How are you different from anyone else you know? List three ways:

1. _____

_____

_____

2. _____

_____

_____

3. _____

_____

_____

Hint: **If you need help, ask a friend or family member what they think is most special about you.**

THE SKIN YOU'RE IN

In Minecraft, you can try on different "skins" or make your character look different ways. In real life, we need to learn to love the skin we're in.

Draw a picture of yourself below. Put a star next to any physical features you love, such as your freckles.

TURN IT AROUND

Have features you don't love? Most people do!
But nothing is all bad.

**Name one thing you don't love, and then turn it
upside down: come up with a reason why that
feature can be good. We'll get you started.**

I'm too green!

But that makes you super sneaky. You blend in with trees and bushes!

A feature you don't love: _____

Why it can be a good thing: _____

_____

_____

Need help? Ask an adult. Was there a feature they didn't
like as a kid that they're actually proud of now?

THE THINGS YOU CAN DO

Confidence comes from knowing your strengths, or what you do well. Maybe you're a good listener or team player. Maybe you're great at soccer or playing piano. Everyone has different strengths, even in Minecraft.

Check off the Minecraft activities that you do well:

- [ ] Mine for blocks
- [ ] Build houses
- [ ] Craft with a crafting table
- [ ] Grow crops
- [ ] Care for animals
- [ ] Tame wolves
- [ ] Build minecart tracks
- [ ] Brew potions
- [ ] Navigate with maps
- [ ] Battle mobs
- [ ] Enchant items
- [ ] Invent with redstone
- [ ] Work together with friends!

ARMED WITH CONFIDENCE

Feeling confident is like wearing enchanted armor. When you know what you like and what you can do, you feel stronger and happier.

Decorate this chest plate with pictures that represent you—your activities, hobbies, and favorite things.

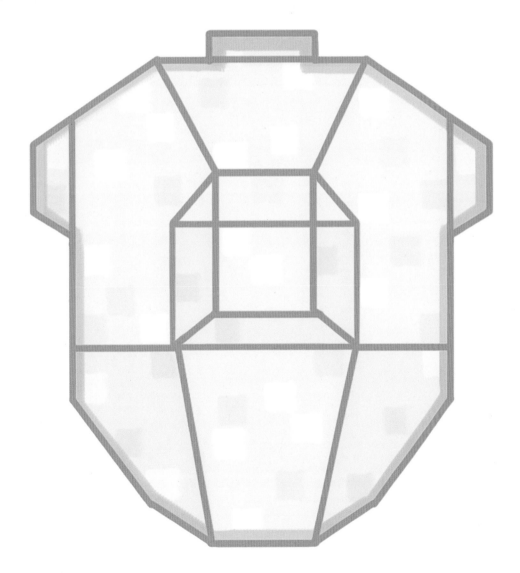

POWERFUL WORDS

Adjectives are words that describe people and things. The words you use to describe yourself have power, so choose them carefully!

Circle the adjectives in this word puzzle, and then draw a star next to the ones that best describe *you*.

WORD LIST:

ATHLETIC
BRAVE
CREATIVE
FRIENDLY
FUNNY
HONEST
KIND
LOYAL
SMART
STRONG

Q V F U N N Y Z W B
H M U M A S G K R R
C S Y F T T T I F A
Z R O O H R J N R V
H S E Z L O U D I E
O M F A E N N A E T
N A Q K T G U G N I
E R S N I I P J D K
S T M K C K V X L E
T L O Y A L K E Y D

POSITIVE POETRY

If you say kind things about yourself, you'll start *feeling* better about yourself too.

Write a poem made up of positive words that start with the letters of your first name. Here's an example:

G: Generous
O: Observant
L: Loyal
E: Energetic
M: Mighty

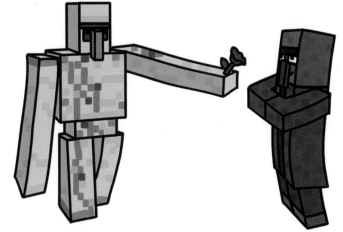

Your turn! Write the letters of your first name in the squares, and come up with positive words that describe you starting with those letters.

WATCH FOR CREEPERS

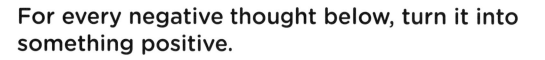

Sometimes unkind thoughts creep into our minds when we're not paying attention. Are you calling yourself names or saying you can't do something? Talk back to that voice in your head!

For every negative thought below, turn it into something positive.

No one wants to be friends with me.

I'm a good friend because _____.

People don't like me.

People like that I _____.

I'll never be good at that.

I'll get better at _____ **if I** _____.

I'm such a loser!

I'm such a good _____.

I can't do it.

I can _____ **if I keep trying.**

WHO'S GOT YOUR BACK?

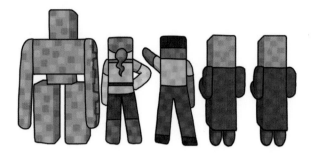

We all need people to rely on.
Think about friends, family members, teachers, coaches, and other people who support you.

How do they make you feel good about yourself? How do you do the same for them?

These are people who help me feel good about myself:

_____ _____ _____

They make me feel appreciated when they _____

_____ .

I make them feel good when I _____

_____ .

Here's something kind someone did for me: _____

_____ .

Here's something I can do to thank them: _____

_____ .

UPS AND DOWNS

Sometimes life feels like riding in a minecart. One day you're at the top of the track, looking out over the world below. The next day, you're zooming downward, hanging on for dear life. You can't control the world around you, but you can control how you react to it.

The next time you have a bad day, rate it on the scale below, with 1 being a not-so-terrible day and 10 being the *worst* day ever.

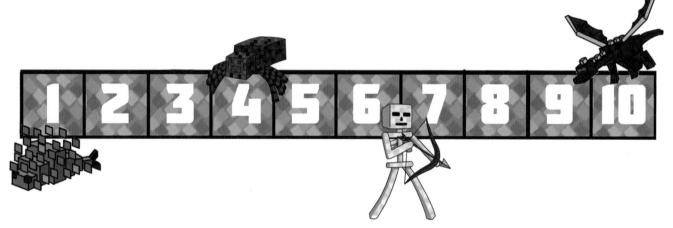

If you rated your bad day a **5 or under**, take a deep breath, give yourself a pep talk, and move on—it'll get better!

If you rated your bad day a **6 or higher**, you may need to get creative to bust out of your bad mood. Try the ideas on the next few pages, and remember this: bad days *always* pass. Tomorrow is a brand-new day!

EXPLORING MOODS

Sometimes our emotions catch us by surprise. We can't prevent every bad mood, but we can figure out ways to feel better.

Think about a time when you were in a good mood. What were you doing? Draw it here:

Can you do this again the next time you're feeling blue?

BAD MOOD BUSTERS

You can't dance your heart out and still be in a bad mood—it's almost impossible! There are lots of ways to boost your mood.

Circle three things that you'll try the next time you're feeling down:

❋ Go outside

❋ Make up a dance

❋ Play with a pet

❋ Talk to a friend or family member

❋ Watch a funny video or show

❋ Play video games with a friend

❋ Take three deep breaths

❋ Write in a journal

❋ Memorize song lyrics

❋ Draw a doodle

TURN UP THE TUNES

Have you ever noticed how music affects your mood? Some songs make you sad or sleepy. Others make you want to get up and *move*.

Make a playlist of songs that make you smile and get your toes tapping. Write the names of the songs here:

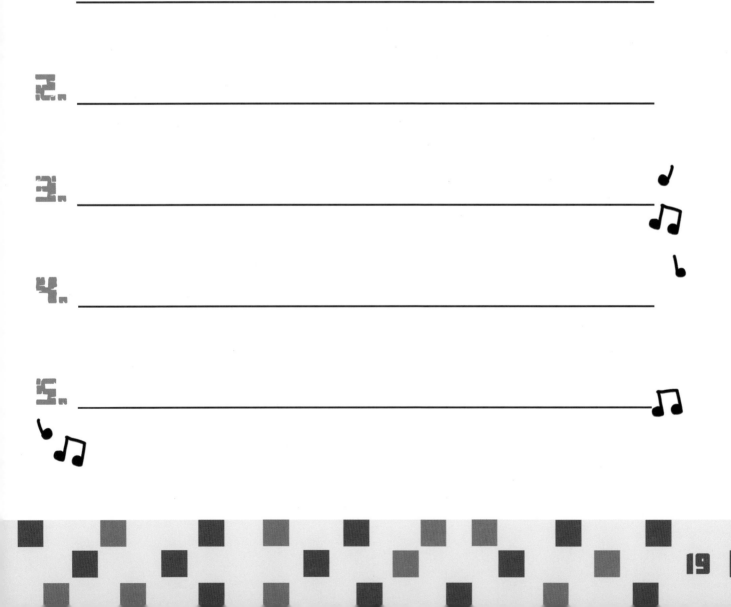

1. _____

2. _____

3. _____

4. _____

5. _____

WHEN STRESS STRIKES

It's hard to feel confident when you're scared or stressed. Are you stressed out? Do you recognize the signs?

Check off anything in the list that sounds like you:

- ☐ My hands feel sweaty a lot.
- ☐ I have trouble sleeping.
- ☐ I get stomachaches every day.
- ☐ I can't catch my breath.
- ☐ I'm always tired.
- ☐ I'm not hungry at mealtime.
- ☐ I snack more than usual.
- ☐ My throat feels tight.
- ☐ My chest feels tight.
- ☐ I get angry easily.
- ☐ I cry often.
- ☐ I can't concentrate at school.

ALL of these can be signs of stress. If you checked **5 or more** boxes, let an adult know that you're feeling stressed. Then keep reading for ways to *stop* stress in its tracks.

HEALTH METER QUIZ

Feeling happy, confident, and stress-free starts with a healthy body. How well are you taking care of your body?

Check the statements that are true about you:

☐ I eat breakfast most days.

☐ I sleep 9 or 10 hours most nights.

☐ I'm active (at recess, in sports, or playing at home) for at least an hour a day.

☐ At dinnertime, I drink water or milk instead of juice or soda.

☐ I take a bath or shower at least two or three times a week.

For every check you made above, color in 2 hearts below.

Now turn the page to see what your health meter is telling you . . .

How did you do?

8 to 10 hearts: You're taking great care of your body! That's the first step to feeling *happy* too.

4 to 6 hearts: You have some healthy habits, but there's more you could do for a healthy body—and mind. Choose one thing from the list that you can try today.

0 to 2 hearts: You're running on empty! Share this checklist with a parent or adult who can help you start taking better care of your body.

DON'T BE A ZOMBIE

If you don't get enough sleep at night, you'll struggle to make it through your day.

Try these tips for getting enough zzz's:

❄ Steer clear of caffeine in the afternoon and evening. No soda or hot chocolate!

❄ Follow the same routine every night, such as taking a shower, brushing your teeth, and reading a book or listening to music.

What's your routine? Write it here:

_____

_____

_____

_____

❄ Once you're in bed, take a few deep breaths. Count to 3 as you inhale, hold the breath for 3 seconds, and count to 3 as you exhale. Imagine that you're breathing in cool confidence and breathing out stress and worry.

A TRIP TO THE OVERWORLD

Can't sleep? Try taking an imaginary trip to your favorite Minecraft setting. Are you fishing at a peaceful pond? Looking out of a tree house high above the jungle floor?

Fill in the blanks below to write a story about your peaceful place.

When I woke up this morning, I wasn't in my bed at all. I'd somehow been transported into the Minecraft Overworld! Luckily, I was in my most favorite place: _____. I could see nothing but _____ for miles around. I could feel the _____ on my face. There was some delicious smell in the air. Was someone making _____? I could taste it already! But for the next few minutes, I decided to sit and enjoy the scenery. I loosened my grip on the _____ in my hands, took a deep breath, and smiled.

Read the story you wrote, and imagine it using *all* of your senses. Now draw the scene in the space below.

Whenever you want to de-stress or worry less, close your eyes and picture yourself in this peaceful place. You don't need a portal to get there!

FROM A TO ZZZ

Sometimes at night, our minds spin like mob spawners. How do you make it stop? Give your brain something else to do.

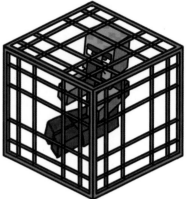

Try the Minecraft alphabet game. For each letter, think of a mob, critter, enchantment, or item that starts with that letter. (You've been given a head start!)

A: <u>Axe</u>

B: _____

C: _____

D: _____

E: _____

F: <u>Fireworks</u>

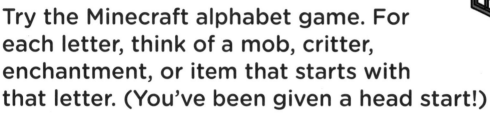

G: _____

H: _____

I: _____

J: _____

K: <u>Knockback enchantment</u>

L: Llama

M: _____

N: _____

O: _____

P: _____

Q: Quartz

R: _____

S: _____

T: _____

U: Unbreaking enchantment

V: _____

W: _____

X: X marks the spot!

Y: _____

Z: _____

Want to play an easier version? The next time you're lying in bed awake at night, try to think of a Minecraft mob, critter, or item for every color in the rainbow. Red **parrots,** orange **lava** . . . and so on!

MESS = STRESS, CLEAN = CONFIDENCE

To feel less stressed and more confident, clean your room! Rearrange it, or decorate it the way you'd decorate a house in Minecraft.

Practice by coloring in the room below, adding each item in this list:

- ✳ A painting on the wall
- ✳ A colorful bedspread
- ✳ A patterned rug
- ✳ Window curtains
- ✳ A soft lamp or torch
- ✳ Flowers

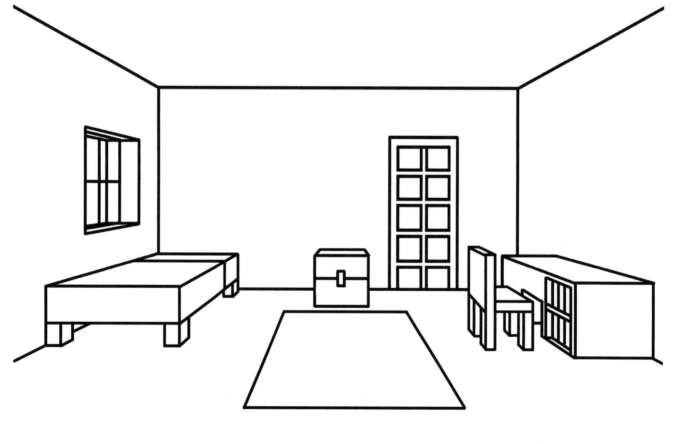

Now try it with your own room. Tidy things up and ask your parents if you can rearrange furniture. Then add some comforting touches, like a cozy blanket or pillows, a framed picture you drew, and photos of your family or friends.

Design your new and improved room in the space below:

GREEN WITH ENVY

Do you ever wish you could run as fast as a friend? Or that you were as creative or as brave? Trying to be like someone else drains your confidence! Get jealous thoughts out of your head by paying that friend a compliment. You'll instantly feel better, and your friend will too.

Need practice? Write a compliment (such as "You're so good at . . ." or "I like the way you . . .") next to each of the mobs below.

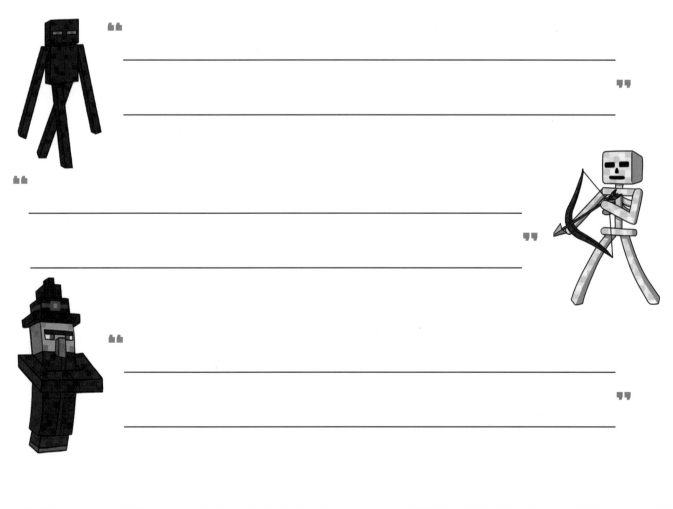

BE-FRIEND YOURSELF

If your confidence starts to slip, give yourself a pep talk—just like you would with a friend. If you practice speaking kindly to yourself, you'll have the words to use whenever you need a boost.

Fill in the blanks below.

[Your name here] _____,

I really like how you _____,

_____, and _____.

You're already good at _____. And you've been

practicing _____, so I know you're

going to get better and better.

[Your name here] _____, you rock!

TEACH A TRICK

Do you know how to do a card trick? How to make amazing hot chocolate? Or how to ride a pig in Minecraft? Teach someone else!

List three skills you have, along with someone—like a friend, sibling, or grandparent—who might want to learn them.

I'll teach these skills . . .

1. _____

2. _____

3. _____

. . . to these people:

1. _____

2. _____

3. _____

LEARN A TRICK

Every time you learn something new, you'll feel more confident too!

Think of three things you'd like to get better at, such as running, drawing, or crafting in Minecraft. Then think of three people who might be able to give you tips.

I'll learn these skills . . .

1. _____

2. _____

3. _____

. . . from these people:

1. _____

2. _____

3. _____

Need help coming up with ideas? Turn to page 38 for tiny goals that'll give you big boosts of confidence.

TONGUE TWISTER CHALLENGE

How did you get better at Minecraft? By playing, trying new things, making a few mistakes, and playing some more. Every small achievement makes it easier to tackle the *next* bigger goal.

Master the tongue twister below. The first time you try it, your tongue might trip. But the more you practice, the better you'll get!

Steve saw one slime swimming and one slime sliding into the swamp. He swung his stone sword and struck a salmon instead.

SKETCH A CREEPER

Learn how to draw a creeper in three easy steps.

First, trace the outline below. Then use the space next to it to draw a creeper of your own. Finally, personalize it. Can you add a hat or an outfit to make it unique, just like you?

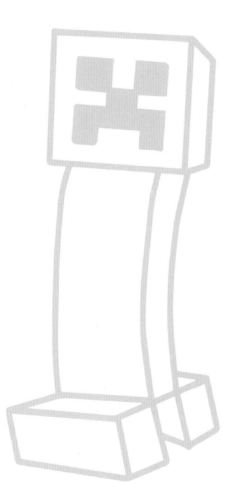

START A STORY

Write a story featuring YOU saving the day by doing something smart or brave.

Can't think of any ideas? Use one of these to kick-start your creativity.

❉ [YOUR NAME HERE] added the final ingredient to the bubbling potion. Night was falling! Would the potion be ready in time?

❉ As the cave spider hissed and crept forward, [YOUR NAME HERE] swallowed hard and grabbed the only weapon within reach . . .

❉ [YOUR NAME HERE] flipped the lever, activating the redstone. The minecart sped forward and rounded a corner, straight into . . .

Write your story here:

_____

_____

_____

_____

_____

_____

_____

_____

_____

_____

Read your story out loud. How does it make you feel?

TACKLE TINY GOALS

Need more fun ways to boost
your confidence?

Check off the things you'd like to try:

☐ Save money for something special. Decorate
a small box to look like a treasure chest and add
a slot on top for gold ingots—er, dollars and coins!

☐ Draw a comic strip featuring you as a superhero or a
master Minecrafter.

☐ Build a house out of playing cards instead of Minecraft blocks.

☐ Map out an obstacle course at a playground that you can do
without touching the ground. (Imagine that you're in the Nether,
and the ground is hot lava!) Time yourself and try to get faster
each time you complete the course.

☐ Taste a food you've never tried before. (Mushroom stew,
anyone?) Take at least three bites.

☐ Make up a tongue twister about spiders spawning in sand.
Add as many "s" words as you can.

AIM HIGH!

Bigger goals take time and effort, but you feel *really* good when you meet them—and ready to tackle the next one on your list. So set your sights high.

What do you want to do? Choose one of these goals, or add your own.

Ace a quiz.

Make a sports team.

Face a fear.

Your goal: _____

Your goal: _____

Your goal: _____

STEPS TO SUCCESS

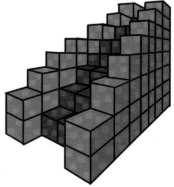

Choose a goal from the previous page, and break it down into small steps. If your goal is to ace a spelling quiz, your steps might look like this:

✷ Set up a study schedule.

✷ Make flash cards.

✷ Find a buddy to practice with.

✷ Practice for 30 minutes every night after school.

✷ Get a good night's sleep before the quiz.

Your turn! What is your goal?

_____

List 5 steps you can take to reach that goal:

1. _____

2. _____

3. _____

4. _____

5. _____

PICK YOUR TEAM

Sometimes reaching goals takes teamwork. Don't be afraid to ask for help!

Think of at least one person for each of the "teammates" below:

❊ The cheerleader who picks me up when I'm

feeling down: _____

❊ The coach who gives me great advice: _____

❊ The teammate who will work hard with me: _____

_____

❊ The friend who makes everything more fun: _____

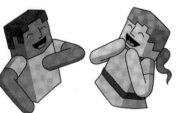

_____

❊ The people who will celebrate with me when I reach my goal:

_____, _____,

and _____

WHAT'S YOUR NEXT MOVE?

Nobody reaches their goal without making mistakes or taking a few wrong turns. That's how you learn and figure out your *next* best move.

Complete the maze below. Every time you take a wrong turn, turn around and try again. You'll get there!

WEBS OF WORRY

Worries are like cobwebs that keep you from moving forward. Are you worried about making mistakes? Not reaching your goal? Embarrassing yourself?

Write the word "So" in front of each of the worries below.

_____ what if I make a mistake?

At least you tried. You probably learned something too, which means you're one step closer to reaching your goal. So get up and keep going!

_____ what if I embarrass myself in front of everyone?

People aren't watching that closely. They have worries of their own. And if they DO see you do something embarrassing? Laugh with them and move on. They'll move on soon too.

_____ what if someone else can do it better?

Reaching your goal isn't about beating anyone else. It's about doing what YOU said you were going to do. The only way you can "lose" is not to try at all.

You just pulled out your "so what?" shears and snipped your worries down to size. Feel better?

MEMORIZE A MOTTO

Keep your confidence flowing with a *motto*, or a saying that makes you feel strong and unstoppable.

Unscramble the words below to read each motto:

1. DON'T W-H-I-S _____ FOR IT.

   K-W-O-R _____ FOR IT!

2. BIG GOALS START WITH L-S-A-M-L _____ STEPS.

3. IF I B-E-V-E-I-E-L _____ I CAN, I WILL.

4. THIS IS T-G-O-U-H _____, BUT SO AM I.

5. I DON'T HAVE TO BE P-C-T-R-E-F-E _____
   TO BE AMAZING.

PICTURE SUCCESS

Imagine what it'll be like when you reach your goal. Are you crossing the finish line of a 5K race? Seeing an "A" at the top of your quiz? Starring in the school play?

In the space below, draw your confident self reaching your goal. Whenever you need a boost, close your eyes and picture that success in your mind too.

WOOT, WOOT!

When you do reach your goal, take time to celebrate!

List three things you'll do to reward yourself and to thank the teammates who helped you get there.

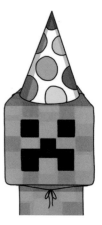

1. _____

_____

_____

2. _____

_____

_____

3. _____

_____

_____

THIS OR THAT?

Ocelots love salmon and wolves love bones. Everyone has likes and dislikes—they make us unique.

Circle the word in each pair that YOU like best, and then share the quiz with a friend. Did you choose different things? Good! Talk about why, and remember: it's *okay* to disagree.

ocelot	OR	wolf
diamonds	OR	emeralds
bow and arrow	OR	sword
minecart	OR	Elytra wings
mooshroom	OR	llama
potion of Invisibility	OR	potion of Water Breathing
Desert Biome	OR	Cold Taiga Biome
iron golem	OR	snow golem
riding a horse	OR	riding a pig
red mushroom	OR	brown mushroom

ONE-OF-A-KIND STYLE

Lots of kids express their personality through the clothes they wear. What's your style?

Design "skins" or outfits for the three figures below, and then star the one you like best.

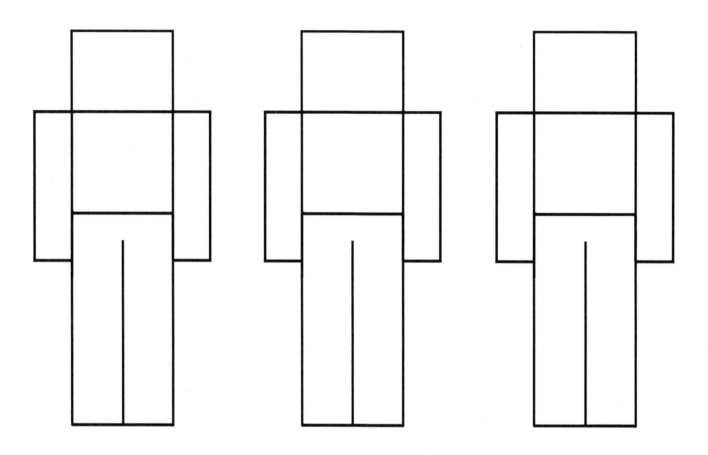

When you choose outfits in real life, don't let other kids tell you what you should or shouldn't wear. Wear what you like. Set your own trends. Who knows? Other kids might start copying YOU!

WHEN SOMEONE TAKES A SHOT

Sometimes kids disagree in a mean way instead of a respectful way. What do you do if someone teases you about what you're wearing? Respond with confidence.

Check off the words below that you could use:

AGREE TO DISAGREE:

☐ That's your opinion.

☐ It's a free country. I'll wear what I want.

MAKE A JOKE:

☐ Aw, you're so sweet!

☐ Hey, thanks for the compliment!

STAY SILENT (WHO SAYS YOU HAVE TO RESPOND?):

☐ Just shrug, smile, and walk away.

SPEAK UP (BEFORE YOU BLOW UP!)

If a friend isn't treating you well, do you stay silent? Or bottle up your anger until you blow sky high? There's a better way to let your friend know how you feel.

• Start with the words "I feel . . ." instead of "You always (do this or that) . . ." That way, your friend won't feel like you're pointing the finger and might be more likely to listen.

• Describe WHEN you feel that way, such as "when you play with other kids and don't invite me." Be specific! Your friend can't read your mind.

• Give your friend a chance to make things better. What do you want your friend to do differently? Try "I'd feel better if you would ask me to join you."

Think of something that's been bothering you. How can you let a friend know what you need? Fill in the blanks below:

I feel _____ when you _____

_____. I would feel better

if you _____ instead.

FRIEND OR FOE?

Does a friend keep saying or doing something hurtful? It's time to decide if this person is *really* a friend.

Check off everything that sounds like your friend below.

My friend . . .

- ☐ Has shared my secrets with other people.
- ☐ Leaves me out of things often.
- ☐ Has called me names.
- ☐ Gets mad if I play with anybody else.
- ☐ Always has to beat me in games.
- ☐ Has said mean things about me behind my back.
- ☐ Teases me about the way I look.

How many boxes did you check?

0 to 2: This friendship may be worth saving. Talk to your friend using the words "I fee . . . when you . . ." Does he or she listen?

3 to 4: This "friend" treats you badly. It's time to take a step back and focus on other friends.

5 to 7: This person is a bully, not a buddy. Steer clear! Turn the page for tips on dealing with bullies.

STANDING UP TO BULLIES

People who bully are trying to take away your power—and confidence.

How do you stop them? Memorize the motto hidden in the secret message below. To decode the message, circle each word that comes right after the word GHAST.

GHAST NOBODY BATTLES GHAST CAN FLY WITH
GHAST TAKE GHAST AWAY FROM THE NETHER
GHAST MY IRON SWORD GHAST POWER FIREBALLS

Write the words you circled here:

_____

_____

Remember this motto the next time you need to stand strong.

A BULLY-PROOF BODY

How confident are you? Your body gives off clues. Kids without confidence might slouch or slump their shoulders. They might hang their head or stare at the ground. But confident kids look like *this:*

Look in the mirror and practice a confident pose. Imagine yourself in enchanted armor, as if nothing anyone says or does can harm you. Can you check off each box?

- [ ] Head high
- [ ] Shoulders back
- [ ] Standing tall
- [ ] Eyes up or straight ahead

When you practice looking confident on the outside, you start *feeling* more confident on the inside. And that'll help you stand up to bullying.

IMAGINE THIS

Ignoring teasing and bullying is harder than it sounds! Tap into your imagination to make it easier.

Circle one answer for each statement below, and then picture it in your mind. The more you practice mind tricks, the easier it is to use them when you need them!

* Pretend the bully is a pesky parrot or a clucking chicken.

* Pretend you just splashed the bully with a potion of Invisibility or Slowness.

* Imagine you are soaring high above the bully with Elytra wings or on the back of the Ender Dragon.

YOUR BACK-UP TEAM

If ignoring a bully doesn't work, it's time to tell an adult what's going on. Who can you talk with?

Check off at least two people below and add names next to them.

☐ Parent: _____

☐ Teacher: _____

☐ School librarian: _____

☐ Coach: _____

☐ Neighbor: _____

☐ Aunt or uncle: _____

☐ Grandparent: _____

If you're facing a bully now, ask for help in person, by phone, or even with a written note. Just *tell* someone. You'll feel better when you have support standing up to bullying.

STANDING UP FOR OTHERS

If you hurt a zombie pigman in Minecraft, what do the other pigmen do? They all come after you! In real life, it's not always easy to stand up for other people. But if enough of you speak up, you can stop bullies in their tracks.

Check off the things you think YOU could do:

☐ Say to the bully, "That's not very funny."

☐ Say to the bully, "You're bullying. Stop it."

☐ Ask the person being bullied, "Are you okay?"

☐ Go stand by the person being bullied.

☐ Say to the person being bullied, "C'mon, let's get out of here."

☐ Invite the person being bullied to hang out with you and your friends.

Practice the words you checked in front of the mirror so that you have them when you need them.

KIND WORDS ♥♥♥♥♥♥♥♥♥

When you're kind to others, it gives you a boost of confidence too.

Unscramble the words below for ways to spread kindness.

Laugh at someone's K-J-E-O _____.

L-E-S-M-I _____ at everyone you meet.

Make a D-C-R-A _____ to thank someone for something they did for you.

Help a family member do his or her
H-R-E-C-O-S _____.

Share a K-S-C-N-A _____ with a friend.

C-O-T-P-M-N-M-L-I-E _____
someone on something they do well.

CARING MAP

Think of people you know at school, in your neighborhood or community, and even at home. Who could use some kindness?

Write at least one name in each area on the map below. How many names can you come up with?

HOME

SCHOOL

COMMUNITY

SPLASH POTIONS OF CONFIDENCE

You use splash potions to heal yourself and others in Minecraft. Imagine that you could do the same thing in real life!

For each potion bottle below, write someone's name and one kind thing you could do to boost their confidence.

NAME:

NAME:

NAME:

What I can do:

What I can do:

What I can do:

_____

_____

_____

_____

_____

_____

_____

_____

_____

Now, armed with your splash potions, can you go out and spread kindness and confidence?

TAKE INVENTORY

As you reach the end of this book, you now have more tips and tools for boosting confidence. Congratulations!

For each tip you've mastered, draw the picture next to it in your inventory below. Can you fill it up?

1. Know what's unique about you, and shine it bright!

2. Practice busting through bad moods.

3. Take care of your body. Eat well and exercise.

4. Don't be a zombie. Get your zzz's.

5. Set goals. Fly high!

6. Snip away at worry. Ask, "So what if . . .

7. Practice looking confident, as if you're wearing enchanted armor.

8. Use your imagination to fight back against bullying.

9. Gain confidence by spreading kindness.

MY INVENTORY:

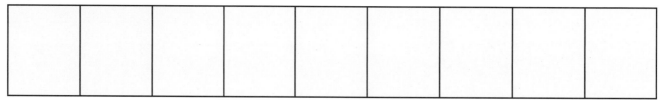

A MOOSHROOM MESSAGE

In Minecraft, mooshrooms are one-of-a-kind and hard to find. This mooshroom has a message for you about confidence.

To decode it, circle only the words that immediately follow the word MOO.

MOO THERE ARE MOO IS A MOO NO MOO ONE MOO IN OUR MOO THE BOX

MOO OVERWORLD NETHER MOO QUITE QUIET MOO LIKE MUSHROOMS

MOO YOU GO MOO SO LLAMAS MOO BE BUSY MOO PROUD OCELOT

MOO OF GUN POWDER MOO WHO GOES MOO YOU ROCK MOO ARE!

Write the words you circled here:

_____

_____

_____

Say them out loud every day. Be confident. Be proud.
Be the one and only YOU!

ANSWER KEY

Page 6

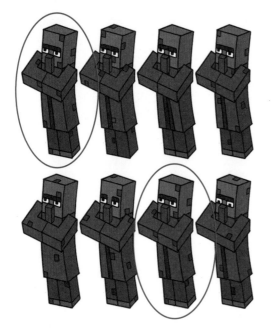

Page 12

Page 42

Page 44

1. DON'T **WISH** FOR IT. **WORK** FOR IT!

2. BIG GOALS START WITH **SMALL** STEPS.

3. IF I **BELIEVE** I CAN, I WILL.

4. THIS IS **TOUGH**, BUT SO AM I.

5. I DON'T HAVE TO BE **PERFECT** TO BE AMAZING.

Laugh at someone's **JOKE**.

SMILE at everyone you meet.

Make a **CARD** to thank someone for something they did for you.

Help a family member do his or her **CHORES**.

Share a **SNACK** with a friend.

COMPLIMENT someone on something they do well.

THERE IS NO ONE IN THE OVERWORLD QUITE LIKE YOU SO BE PROUD OF WHO YOU ARE!